FRANCIS FRITH'S

AROUND EASTLEIGH

LIVING MEMORIES

GORDON DAUBNEY COX was born and educated in Southampton, came to Eastleigh in 1935, and was a school master at the local grammar school. He wanted to know more about his adopted town, joined the local history society and became its Chairman. He encouraged members to undertake research into aspects of the town's past history, and some 100 occasional papers and longer works have been published, many as a result of an annual open competition which still brings in worthwhile entries. Gordon Cox has been deeply involved in town twinning between Eastleigh, Villeneuve-St-Georges and Kornwestheim. He has been made a Citizen of Honour of all three towns, has been honoured with the Palmes Academiques by the French Government, and has received the Phillip Matthaus Hahn Medallion from Germany.

FRANCIS FRITH'S
LIVING MEMORIES

AROUND EASTLEIGH
including Chandler's Ford, Bishopstoke and Botley
LIVING MEMORIES

GORDON DAUBNEY COX

First published in the United Kingdom in 2005 by The Francis Frith
Collection

Hardback Edition 2005 ISBN 1-84589-029-9

Paperback Edition 2005 ISBN 1-84589-053-1

British Library Cataloguing in Publication Data

Around Eastleigh - Living Memories
Gordon Daubney Cox

The Francis Frith Collection
Frith's Barn, Teffont,
Salisbury, Wiltshire SP3 5QP
Tel: +44 (0) 1722 716 376
Email: info@francisfrith.co.uk
www.francisfrith.co.uk

Printed and bound in Great Britain

Front Cover: **EASTLEIGH,** *Leigh Road c1960* E167012t
Frontispiece: **EASTLEIGH,** *Leigh Road c1960* E167002

The colour-tinting is for illustrative purposes only, and is not intended to
be historically accurate

Aerial photographs reproduced under licence from
Simmons Aerofilms Limited.
Historical Ordnance Survey maps reproduced under licence from
Homecheck.co.uk
Every attempt has been made to contact copyright holders of
illustrative material. We will be happy to give full acknowledgement in
future editions for any items not credited. Any information should be
directed to The Francis Frith Collection.

as with any historical database the frith archive is constantly being
corrected and improved and the publishers would welcome information
on omissions or inaccuracies

CONTENTS

FRANCIS FRITH
VICTORIAN PIONEER

FRANCIS FRITH, founder of the world-famous photographic archive, was a complex and multi-talented man. A devout Quaker and a highly successful Victorian businessman, he was philosophical by nature and pioneering in outlook.

By 1855 he had already established a wholesale grocery business in Liverpool, and sold it for the astonishing sum of £200,000, which is the equivalent today of over £15,000,000. Now a very rich man, he was able to indulge his passion for travel. As a child he had pored over travel books written by early explorers, and his fancy and imagination had been stirred by family holidays to the sublime mountain regions of Wales and Scotland. 'What lands of spirit-stirring and enriching scenes and places!' he had written. He was to return to these scenes of grandeur in later years to 'recapture the thousands of vivid and tender memories', but with a different purpose. Now in his thirties, and captivated by the new science of photography, Frith set out on a series of pioneering journeys up the Nile and to the Near East that occupied him from 1856 unti 1860.

INTRIGUE AND EXPLORATION

These far-flung journeys were packed with intrigue and adventure. In his life story, written when he was sixty-three, Frith tells of being held captive by bandits, and of fighting 'an awful midnight battle to the very point of surrender with a deadly pack of hungry, wild dogs'. Wearing flowing Arab costume, Frith arrived at Akaba by camel sixty years before Lawrence of Arabia, where he encountered 'desert princes and rival sheikhs, blazing with jewel-hilted swords'.

He was the first photographer to venture beyond the sixth cataract of the Nile. Africa was still the mysterious 'Dark Continent', and Stanley and Livingstone's historic meeting was a decade into the future. The conditions for picture taking confound belief. He laboured for hours in his wicker dark-room in the sweltering heat of the desert, while the volatile chemicals fizzed dangerously in their trays. Back in London he exhibited his photographs and was 'rapturously cheered' by members of the Royal Society. His reputation as a photographer was made overnight.

VENTURE OF A LIFE-TIME

Characteristically, Frith quickly spotted the opportunity to create a new business as a specialist publisher of photographs. He lived in an era of immense and sometimes violent change. For the poor in the early part of Victoria's reign work was exhausting and the hours long, and people had precious little free time to enjoy themselves. Most people had no transport other than a cart or gig at

their disposal, and rarely travelled far beyond the boundaries of their own town or village. However, by the 1870s the railways had threaded their way across the country, and Bank Holidays and half-day Saturdays had been made obligatory by Act of Parliament. All of a sudden the working man and his family were able to enjoy days out and see a little more of the world.

With typical business acumen, Francis Frith foresaw that these new tourists would enjoy having souvenirs to commemorate their days out. In 1860 he married Mary Ann Rosling and set out on a new career: his aim was to photograph every city, town and village in Britain. For the next thirty years he travelled the country by train and by pony and trap, producing fine photographs of seaside resorts and beauty spots that were keenly bought by millions of Victorians. These prints were painstakingly pasted into family albums and pored over during the dark nights of winter, rekindling precious memories of summer excursions.

THE RISE OF FRITH & CO

Frith's studio was soon supplying retail shops all over the country. To meet the demand he gathered about him a small team of photographers, and published the work of independent artist-photographers of the calibre of Roger Fenton and Francis Bedford. In order to gain some understanding of the scale of Frith's business one only has to look at the catalogue issued by Frith & Co in 1886: it runs to some 670 pages, listing not only many thousands of views of the British Isles but also many photographs of most European countries, and China, Japan, the USA and Canada - note the sample page shown on page 9 from the hand-written Frith & Co ledgers recording the pictures. By 1890 Frith had created the greatest specialist photographic publishing company in the world, with over 2,000 sales outlets - more than the combined number that Boots and WH Smith have today! The picture on the next page shows the Frith & Co display board at Ingleton in the Yorkshire Dales (left of window). Beautifully constructed with a mahogany frame and gilt inserts, it could display up to a dozen local scenes.

POSTCARD BONANZA

The ever-popular holiday postcard we know today took many years to develop. In 1870 the Post Office issued the first plain cards, with a pre-printed stamp on one face. In 1894 they allowed other publishers' cards to be sent through the mail with an attached adhesive halfpenny stamp. Demand grew rapidly, and in 1895 a new size of postcard was permitted called the court card, but there was little room for illustration. In 1899, a year after Frith's death, a new card measuring 5.5 x 3.5 inches became the standard format, but it was not until 1902 that the divided back came into being, so that the address and message could be on one face and a full-size illustration on the other. Frith & Co were in the vanguard of postcard development: Frith's sons Eustace and Cyril continued their father's monumental task, expanding the number of views offered to the public and recording more and more places in Britain, as the coasts and countryside were opened up to mass travel.

Francis Frith had died in 1898 at his villa in Cannes, his great project still growing. The archive he created continued in business for another seventy years. By 1970 it contained over a third of a million pictures *showing 7,000 British towns and villages.*

FRANCIS FRITH'S LEGACY

Frith's legacy to us today is of immense significance and value, for the magnificent archive of evocative photographs he created provides a unique record of change in the cities, towns and villages throughout Britain over a century and more. Frith and his fellow studio photographers revisited locations many times down the years to update their views, compiling for us an enthralling and colourful pageant of British life and character.

We are fortunate that Frith was dedicated to recording the minutiae of everyday life, for it is this sheer wealth of visual data, the painstaking chronicle of changes in dress, transport, street layouts, buildings, housing, engineering and landscape that captivates us so much today. His remarkable images offer us a powerful link with the past and with the lives of our ancestors.

THE VALUE OF THE ARCHIVE TODAY

Computers have now made it possible for Frith's many thousands of images to be accessed almost instantly. Frith's images are increasingly used as visual resources, by social historians, by researchers into genealogy and ancestry, by architects and town planners, and by teachers involved in local history projects.

In addition, the archive offers every one of us an opportunity to examine the places where we and our families have lived and worked down the years. Highly successful in Frith's own era, the archive is now, a century and more on, entering a new phase of popularity. Historians consider the Francis Frith Collection to be of prime national importance. It is the only archive of its kind remaining in private ownership. Francis Frith's archive is now housed in an historic timber barn in the beautiful village of Teffont in Wiltshire. Its founder would not recognize the archive office as it is today. In place of the many thousands of dusty boxes containing glass plate negatives and an all-pervading odour of photographic chemicals, there are now ranks of computer screens. He would be amazed to watch his images travelling round the world at unimaginable speeds through internet lines.

The archive's future is both bright and exciting. Francis Frith, with his unshakeable belief in making photographs available to the greatest number of people, would undoubtedly approve of what is being done today with his lifetime's work. His photographs depicting our shared past are now bringing pleasure and enlightenment to millions around the world a century and more after his death.

THE BOROUGH OF EASTLEIGH
AN INTRODUCTION

TO PEOPLE who do not live in the area, the name of Eastleigh is likely to suggest a railway town in the south of England situated midway between Winchester and Southampton. While it is true that for many years at the beginning of the 20th century it may be said that the railway dominated the lives of its inhabitants, other influences have worked to shape the past, the present and the future of this thriving borough. There are two reasons for the existence of the town of Eastleigh. One is the fact that William Craven, Lord of the Manor of Eastley, was deeply involved in horse racing and had his own stud. He got so hopelessly into debt that he had to sell most of his large estate. The land was bought in 1861 by Thomas Chamberlayne of Cranbury Park, who already owned Barton Manor and land in Bishopstoke.

In due course, he set up an Eastleigh and Bishopstoke Housing Association, and in consultation with Jonas Nichols designed a gridiron pattern of terrace housing for a new town. The other reason for the existence of Eastleigh is that with the growth of a railway network in Britain, it was decided to construct the London & Southampton Railway between Nine Elms (later Waterloo) and a Southampton terminus.

On the way there was to be, in the tithing of Barton, a station which quickly became known as Bishopstoke Junction (Bishopstoke being the nearest village of any size) on account of the lines branching off towards Portsmouth and Salisbury. The first train went through in June 1839. Later, the London & South Western Railway decided to transfer its carriage works (1890) to a neighbouring site, to be followed later by the locomotive works (1910). More houses had to be built for the workers.

As shown by television's Time Team, wherever you dig you are likely to find some sort of relics of the past, and so it is in the Eastleigh district. Not far away to the north of Chandler's Ford can be seen the remains of a large Iron Age fortress dating from about 150 BC; in the centre of it a bishop built a castle - hence the name Merdon Castle. Barrows have been found on Hiltingbury and Cranbury Commons, and some of these burial mounds have been excavated to reveal cremated remains.

Some fifty sites of villas or graves dating from the Roman period have been found, indicating that even in those early days people wished to live away from towns in what was regarded as a pleasant area. There was a large arable plain sloping slowly down to the coast. On the periphery there developed several small settlements or villages (now known as North Stoneham, South Stoneham, Allbrook, Otterbourne, Hursley and Bishopstoke), but in the Eastley area we have a series of small farmsteads (Barton, Boyatt, Allbrook, Ham, Home, North End, and Eastley). In the centre was the River Itchen, which had water mills and water meadows.

As time passed by, monks and others began to record events, and occasionally one finds a written reference to Eastleigh (in various spellings). For instance, there is a Domesday entry for Estleie, which is said to belong to Henry in the place of Godwin who previously held it from King Edward. 'At the time of King Edward it was, as now, worth 40 shillings'. There is an earlier reference to Eastlea in a charter by which King Athelstan granted to the theign Alfred land at North Stoneham in AD 932. Later, a chapel

of Eastlea is recorded in the Deanery of Southampton, and there is an early map of the Southampton Estuary which shows Eastley. Later still, there is the will of William Warley, a farmer of Eastley Farm, who was born in 1588, the year of the Armada, and died in 1649, a few months before the execution of Charles I.

Eastleigh has always been a relatively happy and peaceful place, not greatly affected by troubles found in other local areas. Those who lived in the manor house were Catholics, and therefore subject to the laws of recusancy and suppression that prevailed during the reign of Elizabeth I, but local people were tolerant, and burials were permitted secretly in the churchyard at Twyford. Indeed, there is in the church a wall tablet describing the virtues of Dulcibella Wells. Gilbert Wells did have his possessions confiscated for a while, but they were later restored. His brother Swithun, known as the schoolmaster,

EASTLEIGH, *Market Street, c1955* E167001

undoubtedly helped smuggle foreign-trained Catholic priests into hiding places in England. Although there were agricultural riots in the early 19th century over most of southern England, caused by the introduction of machinery into farming, there were no risings locally. The coming of the railway in 1839 was welcomed by thousands lining the route from Southampton to Winchester, despite the creation of embankments and cuttings which interfered with farming and rural communications.

This, then, can be regarded as the first phase of the history of Eastleigh, a happy rural area, which lasted with comparatively little change until about the end of the 19th century, when the railway factories arrived to alter the face of the slowly growing village and increase the population from roughly 500 to 5000. They came from London, they came from the Isle of Wight, they came from many places in Hampshire and they needed somewhere to live. Hence the rapidly constructed terraces, well built nevertheless, using bricks made from the excellent brick-earth clay found in quantity below the topsoil. In passing, it may be said that locally made bricks and tiles have gone to many places in England and beyond. Indeed, they are still fetching high prices when retrieved from buildings being demolished.

The population continued to increase, settling at about 30,000. For many years the majority of people living in Eastleigh and Bishopstoke were employed by the railway, and some excellent locomotives were produced here. One of the finest, the Lord Nelson, is now being painstakingly restored in the hope of running it again on the local network. A smaller one, the 828, has already been restored and reused. One alternative source of employment for local people in the young town arose from the building of a Pirelli factory in Southampton in 1912. The directors persuaded the farmer at Eastleigh Farm, who was named Nutbeem, to allow the use of some of his fields for sport. In the 1920s, these fields had another factory built on them for the production of submarine cables, providing work for several thousand inhabitants.

An Act of Parliament of 1894 meant that Eastleigh separated from South Stoneham and became an Urban District with its own council, which first met on 5 January 1895. It was a lively council which rapidly set about converting rural conditions - muddy roads, no street lighting and lack of water and sewage services - into an urban setting with paved tree-lined streets, gas lighting, a water supply and sewage disposal. At first, the people of Bishopstoke refused to join with Eastleigh, but when they saw the improvements they accepted the proposal for an Eastleigh and Bishopstoke District Council, as indicated over the original entrance to the council offices. These were built in 1899, and an attractive town hall was added to them in 1928. The council has since moved to new premises, and this building has now become an entertainments venue and is renamed The Point.

Chandler's Ford was separated from Eastleigh by Monks Brook, which was crossed by a ford from Leigh Road into North End Road. In 1932, a bridge was constructed over the stream, the whole road became Leigh Road, and, despite some vigorous opposition, Chandler's Ford was added to the District of Eastleigh. In 1936, a petition for borough status was accepted by the Government and granted by Edward VIII.

During the years of the Second World War, both the railway works and Pirelli's played their part and suffered slight damage from air raids. Elsewhere in the town, houses were bombed and a comparatively small number of persons killed. Those who were young at the time remember low-flying aircraft machine-gunning streets in the centre of the town; some say the pilots all had Hitler-type moustaches.

After the end of the war, the idea spread of twinning between towns in Europe to encourage better knowledge between foreigners. Villeneuve-St-Georges, a town about 9 miles south of Paris, was suggested as a suitable twin town; after preliminary visits, an agreement was reached and a document signed with the aim of encouraging friendship between citizens in the two towns. Villeneuve was already twinned with a town in Germany, Kornwestheim, not far from Stuttgart, and it was natural that eventually Eastleigh would join to form a tripartite partnership. At the time, all three towns were of approximately the same size, and were railway-based with large marshalling

yards. The twinning has been a great success, with large numbers of people making exchanges as individuals or in organised groups. A few international weddings have taken place. All three towns have been awarded the Flag of Honour of the Council of Europe for their successful twinning activities. One unique feature of the twinning is that in November on Commemoration Day the mayors of all three towns (or their deputies) join together for the memorial proceedings in each of the three towns.

In 1974, the act for the reorganisation of local government led to the addition of seven villages taken from the Rural District of Winchester and a considerable increase in population. It was becoming obvious that employment in the railway works was being run down, so the council encouraged the development of small industrial undertakings on a number of sites throughout the borough. With the more recent closure of the Pirelli factory, and the threatened closure of the one-time thriving railway works (now owned by the French Alstom Company), the

EASTLEIGH, *Price's Bakery c1955* ZZZ04130 (Gordon Daubney Cox)

growth of such small industries has been a lifeline for employment, leading to one of the lowest figures for jobseekers in the country and attracting people from neighbouring towns. It is encouraging to note that diverse polls have shown that Eastleigh is one of the best places in the country in which to live. Very large housing developments are now taking place all over District No.9. As part of the many indications of progress in the borough, one may cite the extremely successful recycling programmes which have earned a number of national awards. Of course, there are splendid road, rail and air communications, and the airfield, now known as Southampton International Airport, has reached its limit of capacity.

The first school in Eastleigh was opened in 1870 shortly after the consecration of the parish church. Further schools were provided as the town developed, all originally named after the road in which they were sited. The standard of education has been consistently good, with very few lapses. At present, Eastleigh schools hold a high position in the modern league tables. A feature often commented upon is the main-tenance in the present Sixth Form College of the friendly atmosphere, the strict but fair discipline and high aims set by Miss Annie Smith, founder of the Eastleigh Pupil Teacher Centre in 1904. After 100 years, that institution, starting with 16 pupils, now has over 2000 students.

During the predominance of the railway industries, the inhabitants of Eastleigh were well trained as apprentices and then subject to strict discipline in the shops. They worked long hours. Nevertheless, they had time for and indulged in entertainment and recreation. The Railway Company provided clubs for the workers; in the Institute were a library, a dance hall, a stage, a technical school and rooms for hire. There was also a sports field with an embanked cycle track. The Cooperative Movement prevailed, and there was a strong Temperance Society. Both had their bands, and held frequent processions through the town. Indeed, there were numerous bands, all vying to perform on the bandstand during the week. In 1887, a carnival was started which has continued ever since; today it is held for a week in August, ending with a long procession through the old town. From 1911 onwards there was a Palace of Varieties and also a Picture House with twice nightly shows, which both converted into cinemas after the First World War. There were opportunities for sporting activities of all kinds - athletics, cricket, football (association and rugby), tennis and hockey. There was a recreation ground in the centre of the town, and later a larger sports area in Fleming Park. There was a billiard hall, and in 1933 an open air swimming pool was constructed. Before then, swimmers had used the River Itchen, to the annoyance of those with fishing rights.

In general, the inhabitants of Eastleigh have kept to themselves and fought shy of publicity. However, there are many who have achieved national and international fame. Perhaps one of the most well known is Tommy Green, who won a gold medal in the 1932 Olympic Games at Los Angeles. Vince Hawkins was twice British middle-weight boxing champion, winning the Lonsdale Belt. George Wright was captain of the British bowls team in 1978, Alan Drayton was a decathlon bronze medal winner, and a road has been named after him. It is sad (or should we be proud) that we have a martyr, an intelligent schoolmaster, who lived in Eastley

Manor House, but also had a home in Holborn; here he was apprehended as a practising Catholic, and he was executed in December 1591. Another dweller in the manor house was Maria Fitzherbert, who, after repeated proposals, eventually agreed to marry the Prince of Wales, later George IV. Georgina Smythe was wooed by (but rejected) the son of Louis Philippe, who called her the prettiest girl in England. In 1844, she married a French nobleman and became the Duchesse de la Force; after her death in 1867, she was buried in the cemetery at Crèteil, south of Paris.

Richard St Barbe Baker, who founded the Men of the Trees, was born in West End, and there is now a plaque to him in the centre of the village. There is also a plaque on the house at 146 High Street to commemorate the fact that Noel Croucher was born there. His father died when he was two years old, and then it was 'rags to riches'. He became the richest man in Hong Kong, and used his wealth to set up the Croucher Foundation to enable poor but able students to have a university education. In Eastleigh, there have been musicians a-plenty. They include David Campbell, said to be the finest clarinet player of our generation; Andrew Ball, pianist and judge at the Leeds Music Festival; Jane Parker-Smith, one-time resident organist at the Albert Hall; Melanie Armitstead, leading soprano for the Kent Opera Company; and many others. Perhaps one may mention here Bill Woodrow, trustee of Tate Modern Art Gallery, who was honoured recently by having his sculpture on the fourth plinth in Trafalgar Square, London.

On a more frivolous note, there is Benny Hill;

BOTLEY, *The Mills c1950* B544006

he started his career in Eastleigh, and based his song 'The Fastest Milkman in the West' on his experiences while working at Hann's Dairy. Jane (Crystabel Drewry), pin-up girl of the Daily Mirror, was born in the centre of the town. Other local people have appeared on the London stage, and a few have indulged in car racing, but it is impossible to mention them all here. However, photos and tributes to 11 sportsmen of Eastleigh may be seen in the Activities Room at Fleming Park.

In recent years, the borough council has thought fit to erect a statue of a railwayman on the edge of the Leigh Road pedestrian precinct, and the Fire and Rescue Service has followed with two statues at their Hampshire headquarters further up in Leigh Road. A model Spitfire aeroplane on a roundabout near the airport records the fact that R J Mitchell's prototype first flew from Eastleigh; during the Second World War, after the bombing of the Supermarine factory in Southampton, parts made in museums, halls and huts were assembled and the planes flight-tested in Eastleigh before going into action. The war memorial in the recreation ground is almost unique. Only one other such monument surmounted by an Angel of Victory is known to exist (at Islington in London). It has been announced that Eastleigh Borough Council has accepted a proposal to consider erecting plaques to commemorate some of the famous people of Eastleigh, possibly Sir David Price, Eastleigh's first Member of Parliament, who remained so for 35 years, and Alderman Quilley, first Labour Chairman of the Hampshire Education Committee and of the National Association of Education Committees. Who knows?

Thus, then, we end our brief story of the development from an Eastley farmstead with 80 people in 1841 to the Borough of Eastleigh with 115,000 inhabitants in 2001 - and still growing.

CHANDLER'S FORD, *Hiltingbury/Kingsway Crossroads 1964* C490031

EASTLEIGH

Eastleigh is a place ideally situated for starting or ending a journey by air, rail, road or sea. A short journey to Portsmouth or Southampton gives access to cross-Channel or cross-Atlantic voyages, although sea routes are rapidly diminishing; departures from Southampton of large liners are mostly for cruises, long around-the-world ones or short ones to the West Indies. Both the M3 and M27 motorways pass through the town, allowing rapid access to London and the south coast, east and west. Similarly, there are two railway stations, one in the centre of the town, which has served millions over the years since 1839, and one (Southampton Parkway) at the airport, which has replaced the former grass-covered platforms used as occasional halts. Travel by air has become so popular and convenient that the airfield in Eastleigh, managed by British Airways and now named Southampton International Airport, has reached capacity.

THE AIRPORT *c1960* E167025

This photograph shows a Cessna aircraft as used by the Hampshire Aeroplane Club in front of an early terminal building, with the control tower and a large hangar on the right. Also to be seen on the left ready for action is a rather primitive fire engine.

THE AIRPORT *c1960*
E167026

This is a similar picture to E167025, page 17, but this time with a Jersey Airlines plane (a DC4, the workhorse of post-war air transport). Staff are bringing a gangway and a luggage trolley, apparently after the arrival of the aircraft. The original grass runways have been reconstructed in concrete and lengthened to take larger aircraft.

◄ **THE AIRPORT**
c1960 E167030

Again we see a Jersey Airlines plane, this time being refuelled and prepared for departure. The route from Eastleigh to the Channel Islands was formerly the most popular journey from the airport with 80% of air traffic. That figure is now down to 20% as a result of the introduction of many new national and international routes by other airlines.

◄ **THE AIRPORT**
c1960 E167032

Several aircraft are await-
ing servicing and departure,
indicating the growing
importance of the airport. It
was originally on the fields
of North Stoneham Farm
where Eric Moon landed a
light aircraft in 1910. Since
then it has been used by Sir
Alan Cobham's Flying Circus,
air refuelling bases, the
Hampshire Flying Club and,
in 1918, by the USNAF. In the
centre of the picture can be
seen one of the large hangars
built specially to house aircraft
of the USA flying base. They
remained in use until recently.

NORTH STONEHAM CHURCH
c1960 E167008

Not far from the airport is North Stoneham Church, which has undergone many alterations since it was first built in the 10th century. There are many monuments in the church and in the graveyard to famous people, including Sir Thomas Fleming, who was the Lord Chief Justice who authorised the execution of Guy Fawkes, and Admiral Lord Hawke, victorious in the Battle of Quiberon Bay. In the graveyard are stones bearing indications of the profession of the person buried beneath, such as a violin or books. The ten bells in the tower are often tolled.

BRAMBRIDGE *c1985* ZZZ04121 (Gordon Daubney Cox)

Brambridge, the manor house of Eastleigh, is now in the Winchester District. It is sited off the old road from Eastleigh to Winchester via Allbrook and Twyford. The lodge gates are still there, and it is from this road that the famous double avenue of lime trees can be seen. The house dates from the 16th century, but it has been much altered. It is now approached from Kiln Lane as shown here.

THE STATUE OF SWITHUN WELLS *1990* ZZZ04136 (Gordon Daubney Cox)

Swithun Wells lived in the manor house of Eastley at a time when Catholics were heavily restricted. Mass was illegally celebrated in a house he owned in Holborn, and he was executed in 1591. In 1970 he was one of 40 English martyrs who were canonised. This statue is in the church of St Etheldreda in London, near where Wells was hanged.

▼ LEIGH ROAD

c1960 E167018

We are now in the centre of Eastleigh; in fact, we are looking from the station along Leigh Road, originally a farm track but steadily improved and extended as the town grew. All the main banks are situated here. The National Provincial (left) has become NatWest; the Midland is next door, now HSBC; and the tall building on the right was originally the Wilts and Dorset Bank, which became Lloyds in 1914. The building has been completely rebuilt. The smaller Barclays Bank, seen here on the right, is still next to Lloyds, but has gone round the corner out of sight.

▶ LEIGH ROAD

c1960 E167002

This view is from the foot-way outside Lloyds Bank. On the right is what was once the most important building in the town: the Railway Institute, built by the directors of the railway. It provided a clubroom, a dance hall, a stage, a library and training facilities for young people. It was demolished some years ago and replaced by a Safeways store. On the other side of the road is a men's clothing store, Baker's, and the Eagle Building accommodating Woolworths.

◄ LEIGH ROAD
c1960 E167012

We are now further along Leigh Road and looking back towards the station. Trees planted c1900 are now mature, and more modern lighting has been installed. On the right is the Eagle Building, erected c1900 by William Wallis, an entrepreneur who liked large buildings. It was occupied mainly by Woolworths, but there were also small shops such as the Luton Hat Shop; Alfred Webb, a photographer; Collins, a butcher; and Bayliss, a greengrocer and florist. The edge of the recreation ground can be seen on the left.

► LEIGH ROAD
c1950 ZZZ04122
(Gordon Daubney Cox)

This is the Leigh Road pedestrian precinct between the High Street and Market Street. The railway station can be seen in the distant centre. The tall building on the left is Lloyds Bank, and one can just discern on the right the pinnacles of Woolworths.

LEIGH ROAD *c1960* E167012x

Here we have a close-up of the Eagle Building, so called on account of the 8ft-wide eagle in terra-cotta placed at the top. Built by William Wallis at the turn of the century it was a remarkable feature in a town of only about 5000 people. It was acquired by Woolworths who, sad to say, were given permission to demolish the three central sections in order to expand. The two outside structures can still be seen.

MARKET STREET
c1955 E167001

As the population grew, more shops were needed. Those in Southampton Road near the station became insufficient, and houses in Market Street were converted, usually by extending out over the small front garden. Major provision merchants such as Lipton, Maypole, International and Gregg set up

premises which are now replaced by Tesco and Safeways. In 1936, Montague Burton came to open a new building. It is still there (right). Note the Regal Cinema on the left and just the edge of the Picture House opposite.

MARKET STREET *c1960* E167015

This is a slightly later view than E167001. Baker's is still on the corner. On the opposite corner is Smith Bradbeer & Co Ltd, a well-supported local general clothing and furniture store. Note that one of the cinemas, the Picture House, has given way to Fine Fare (centre right). A particular feature of these early days was the sun-blinds to be seen out over the footway in the centre of the picture. Their purpose was to shield the copious provisions in shop windows.

▼ **MARKET STREET** *c1965* E167044

We are looking in the opposite direction from E167015, page 25, along Market Street. Burton's is pre-eminent on the left, and Pricerite is on the right, next to three shoe shops, Lennard's, True-Form and Frisby's. All have gone. The Wilts & Dorset Bank building is in the distant centre, towering over the roof of the parish church at the far end.

▶ **HIGH STREET**

c1955 E167019

Further development of the town meant further conversion of houses into shops. Note that Smith Bradbeers has moved to this corner, from Market Street (see page 25). Note also the roofline, with chimneys and upper rooms above the shops in the centre. The land on which the original Eastleigh was built belonged to Thomas Chamberlayne, and he gave the new streets names associated with his family and estate. The High Street was first given the name of his son, Tankerville.

◄ HIGH STREET
c1960 E167020

This photograph shows the shops on the other side of the street from E167019. On the comer (right) we have Delbridges. The nearest building on the right was originally Lloyds Bank. In 1914 it became a private school run by two ladies named Gamlen. In 1936 Barton's, seed merchants, moved here, but were eventually bought out by the Delbridge family; grandfather, son and grandson all served in the shop. It has now become Kentucky Fried Chicken. Note the Hants & Dorset bus; certainly no such traffic is allowed now in the one-way street.

► THE TOWN HALL
c1960 E167022

The Urban District Council of 1895 needed a home, and in 1899 the council offices were built and occupied. In 1928 it was decided to add a town hall and modify the western end of the building. The new part is at the left-hand side of the picture; it was a popular place for all sorts of community activities. Beyond the town hall there is a glimpse of the trees surrounding the recreation ground. It is very sad that many of the trees on the right were felled by the gales of 1987.

► **THE LIBRARY** *c1960*
E167021

Eastleigh Library, built in 1936, provided a welcome addition for the people of Eastleigh. It was well stocked with books, and soon became too small for the needs of the population. When the Swan Centre was built, the library moved to occupy a site on the first floor, since when the issue of books has increased and provisions for modern technology have made it a busy place. To the right of this picture can be seen houses in Archer's Road, part of the development of Newtown in c1910.

◀ **THE RECREATION GROUND** *c1960*
E167041

The recreation ground was part of Little Eastleigh Farm. It became known as the cricket field, and in due course was bought by the Urban District Council. In the distant centre can be seen a house named Fairholme, the home of William Panter, superintendent of the carriage works and a leading man in the early development of the new town. The bandstand dates from 1909; it has a concrete base and roof replacing an earlier open wooden structure. In the centre is the war memorial, almost unique with its angel of victory; there is only one other such memorial in England. Just visible on the left is part of the library.

detail of E167041

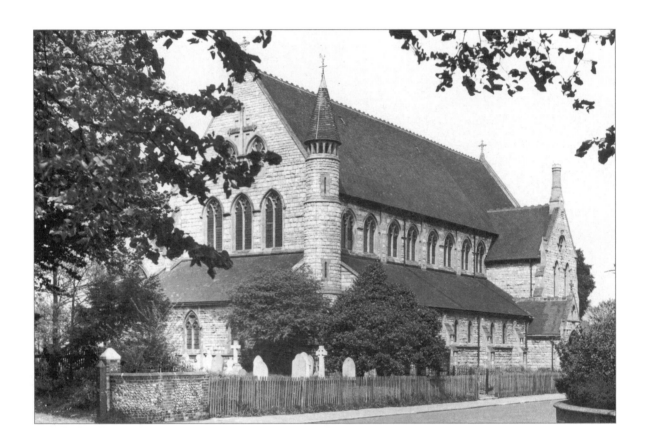

THE PARISH CHURCH *c1955* E167003

Eastley was a tithing in the large parish of South Stoneham, which was where births, marriages and deaths had to be registered. After the opening of a railway station in the neighbouring tithing of Barton (the station was called Bishopstoke after the nearest village of any size), the growing population petitioned the Government for a church of their own. In December 1868, the Queen in Council created a new ecclesiastical parish of Eastleigh; the name with its new spelling had been suggested by Charlotte Yonge, the authoress who lived in nearby Otterboume, and who made a large contribution to the cost of the new church. It was designed by G E Street, the architect of the Palace of Justice in London. After being declared redundant, the church has lately been converted into flats.

THE PARISH CHURCH ON FIRE *1985* ZZZ04125 (Used by courtesy of Reg Vince)

Eastleigh Parish Church of the Resurrection was declared redundant many years ago, and All Saints' Church further south had taken over. On Sunday 21 July 1985 a fire broke out which almost completely destroyed the building. Most of the walls remained, and flats have been constructed within the listed building.

THE SWIMMING POOL *c1955* E167316

We now leave the old tithing of Eastley and come over the London to Southampton railway line into Barton. In 1932, the local County High School left the Barton Peveril farmhouse (which gave it its name), and shortly afterwards this open air swimming pool was built in the grounds. Water from the Barton River was filtered through the chlorination plant at the far end, left centre.

▶ **THE SAFEWAY SUPERMARKET** *c1995*
ZZZ04123 (Gordon Daubney Cox)

The Safeway supermarket, recently purchased by Morrisons, stands here on the site of the former Railway Institute. The road to the right is Upper Market Street, once known as Park View. Bus departure points lie along the side of the building.

THE SWIMMING POOL *c1960* E167035

As can be seen, the Eastleigh swimming pool was very popular. Many galas were organised, and schools used it for their swimming training and sports. Fishermen were particularly pleased with this development, hoping that the pool would be used by those people who previously swam in the River Itchen and disturbed their activities.

HOME FARM
c1990 ZZZ04128
(Gordon Daubney Cox)

Home Farm, opposite the railway station, dates from the 16th century and is one of the few buildings listed in the 1841 census of Eastley. It has been much improved since the time when it had a thatched roof, but is still an important feature of Eastleigh.

33

COMMEMORATIVE PLAQUE *c1990* ZZZ04134 (Gordon Daubney Cox)
When Burton's clothing shop came to Eastleigh in 1936, Montague Burton performed the opening ceremony. This stone, which commemorates the fact, is at the base (left-hand side) of the shop in Market Street.

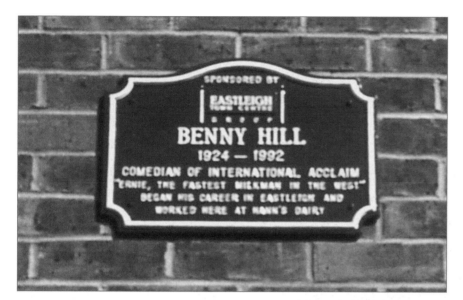

THE BENNY HILL PLAQUE *c2000* ZZZ04135 (Gordon Daubney Cox)

Although born in Southampton, the comedian Benny (real name Alfred) Hill worked at Hann's Dairy and started his career in an Eastleigh concert party. This plaque is near the entrance to the dairy where he worked as a milk delivery man, an experience which inspired his song about Ernie the milkman, who drove the fastest milk-cart in the west.

THE PIRELLI FACTORY *c1980* ZZZ04124 (Gordon Daubney Cox)

This is the great wall of the Pirelli factory, which was recently demolished and replaced by over 900 homes. During the Second World War the wall was camouflaged to look like houses on the opposite side of the road, and the camouflage remained visible until the building's demolition.

▶ **THE STATUE OF A FIREMAN** *c2000*
ZZZ04133 (Gordon Daubney Cox)

This statue of a fireman has been erected in the grounds of the Hampshire Fire and Rescue Services in Leigh Road. It is proposed to have two more statues near the main entrance to the headquarters.

◀ **THE FORMER NORTH END SCHOOL** *c1950*
ZZZ04127 (Gordon Daubney Cox)

The former North End School, built in 1939, was later purchased from the Hampshire Education Committee by the Hampshire Fire and Rescue Services - it is now their headquarters.

▲ **THE FORMER CRANBURY ROAD INFANTS SCHOOL** *c1995*
ZZZ04126 (Gordon Daubney Cox)

The former Cranbury Road Infants School on the left is now used by Eastleigh College.
The building on the right stands on the site of the All Saints Mission Hall, dating from 1900. It later became known as Centre 66. After it was destroyed by fire, was replaced by the attractive edifice seen here, now named Cranbury Community Centre.

◀ **THE CONSTITUTIONAL CLUB** *c1990* ZZZ04129
(Gordon Daubney Cox)

The Constitutional Club, built in 1901, is the only building of distinction remaining from that period of elegant buildings in Eastleigh. It is used as the Conservative Party Headquarters, but has changed its name to Churchill's.

▶ **FLEMING PARK**
The Miniature Golf Course c1955 E167007

From the start in 1895, successive councils have sought to provide facilities for recreation. In 1929 the council negotiated the purchase, at a very reasonable figure, of a large area of land owned by the Fleming family, who were the patrons of North Stoneham, and it was named Fleming Park. The pavilion in this picture was built together with a rose garden and a fountain, all perfectly managed by Harry Thornton, the ideal groundsman. In the foreground is a miniature golf course. The row of houses is in Passfield Avenue, so named after a Labour Party peer of the time.

PRICE'S BAKERY
c1955 ZZZ04130
(Gordon Daubney Cox)

Price's was one of a number of small bakeries in Southampton. It grew steadily, and settled as a major bakery in Eastleigh. Now one of a large combine, its days are numbered. It has been announced that 'Mr Kipling's Exceedingly Good Cakes' will no longer be made here after the end of 2005.

FLEMING PARK
The Putting Green
c1955 E167023

Here we have another view of the pavilion and miniature golf course at Fleming Park, where there were also football, rugby and hockey pitches and tennis courts. Within the last twenty years a new pavilion has been built, a large sports hall added, and an indoor swimming pool provided. Further improvements are planned, including all-weather pitches. There is also a children's pool and play area.

THE WAR MEMORIAL *c1965* ZZZ04131 (Gordon Daubney Cox)

The charming war memorial in the recreation ground is surmounted by the Angel of Victory.
Some years ago she was stolen; but recently she has been replaced, and her two feet embedded in concrete.
There is only one other similar monument in England, in Islington, London.

THE RAILWAYMAN STATUE BY JILL TWEED *1995* ZZZ04132 (Gordon Daubney Cox)

Some time ago, the Eastleigh Borough Council decided to erect a statue. A short list of three possibilities was put on display, and the public were invited to choose. There was an 80% vote in favour of the railwayman by Jill Tweed in preference to a Spitfire or a modern-style statue.

BISHOPSTOKE

Bishopstoke – its name indicates that it was a settlement owned by the Bishop of Winchester - has a long history. It seems certain that there was a Saxon church here, and that the village suffered when the Danes invaded the lands around the Southampton estuary fed by the rivers Test and Itchen. There are maps dating from 1618 showing how the rural nature of the area slowly changed, giving way first to a collection of large houses in their spacious grounds; these were favoured by gentry (including one Admiral Kepple) on account of the area's pleasant hilly nature overlooking the river Itchen. There was a further attraction when the London to Southampton railway line was laid nearby, with a station which for many years was known as Bishopstoke Junction. Later there was a major change when the railway factories arrived, first for carriages and wagons, and then for steam locomotives. Some of the grounds were sold, and gradually housing estates were established; while these added considerably to the population, they nevertheless did not destroy the friendly community spirit in the village - which, indeed, is still there. More recently, the area of Old Bishopstoke along the banks of the river has been declared a Conservation Area. At the time of writing there is considerable concern about a large house and grounds stretching down to the river called The Mount, once owned by a benevolent gentleman named Cotton. The house became a hospital, and a number of extensions were built, but the National Health Service has now closed the hospital and is about to sell the property.

BISHOPSTOKE, *The River Itchen c1960* B693029

Beyond the tithing of Barton and after crossing water meadows, we come to the pretty village of Bishopstoke. This photograph has been taken from the left bank of the River Itchen, and the photographer appears to have been standing on a spot where there was once a ford - children played there even after the bridge was built. On the right is the old mill house, now converted into flats. Left centre, just beyond the van, is a glimpse of the Prince of Wales public house.

BISHOPSTOKE
The River Itchen c1950
E167010

This view has been taken from the right bank of the river. Eastleigh is to the left, and Fair Oak to the right. The car is turning out of Riverside (formerly Mill Road), which leads to the older part of the village. There was once a huge mill here, long since gone. The terrace of houses on the right is part of a development built at the end of the 19th century.

BISHOPSTOKE, *The Village c1955* B693002

We have turned into Riverside, a delightful waterside road. On the right is the Anchor Inn, at this time owned by the brewers Strong & Co of Romsey. It has now been converted into flats and a doctor's surgery. We have reached the era of fish and chips, wrapped in newspaper and eaten possibly in the street or in Smart's Fried Fish Saloon (right).

▼ BISHOPSTOKE
Riverside c1965 B693050

Here we are looking south. There were two inns in Riverside, the Anchor, still a prominent feature although the front has been reconstructed, and the Anglers, affectionately known to locals as the Annie Miles, the name of the lady manager in 1900 – the nickname is still in use today. In the distance can be seen a small shopping centre with a post office at the point where Spring Lane branches off from Riverside.

▶ BISHOPSTOKE
Spring Lane c1955
B693003

Spring Lane, originally called Back Lane, branches off from Riverside and can be seen at the top centre turning back into the main road. This is the centre of the old village. Next to the post office (right) is the old Methodist church, now replaced by a new building. Near here is a butcher's shop over which early Methodists once met. The present butcher is famous as a national prize-winner for making sausages.

◄ **BISHOPSTOKE**
Spring Lane c1955
B693026

This is a closer view of Spring Lane. Although all the buildings on the left have been replaced by flats, the road remains narrow and attractive. Shops are still thriving, and one tradesman reckons to sell everything that might be bought in a general ironmonger's.

► **BISHOPSTOKE**
The Old Church c1960
B693022

This is the ivy clad tower remaining from a church built in 1823, most of which was demolished in 1909. The tower was taken down shortly after this photo was taken. The site of the church is now marked out in stones and there is a memorial table. The graveyard has become a pleasant open space. A new and bigger church was built on another site (see page 48).

BISHOPSTOKE
*St Mary's Church
c1960* B693052

This is the new
St Mary's Church built
in 1891 to replace the
older building.
Mr Barton gave the
land and £1,000
towards the cost on
condition that there
should be no pew
rents as there had
been in the older
church. The tower was
added as a memorial
to Admiral Kepple,
who had lived in the
village and was a
church warden. There
is a peal of ten bells.

BISHOPSTOKE, *Montague Terrace c1955* B693006

At Bishopstoke the River Itchen divides into a number of waterways. There are two mill streams, one known as the Barton
River, from which water is provided for the Itchen Navigation Canal, and this branch, which follows the Fair Oak Road with
Montague Terrace on the right of the picture. All the streams rejoin the river further south. The house left centre was
St Agnes, and became a doctor's surgery. The River Inn has now been built there.

BISHOPSTOKE, *Fair Oak Road c1960* B693031

We are on the Fair Oak Road, but here looking back towards Eastleigh. The No 43 bus (the front one) was a service between Bishop's Waltham and the airport via Bishopstoke and Eastleigh. Hants & Dorset buses in their green livery have been replaced by Solent Blue. On the left can be seen a field of a farm which no longer exists.

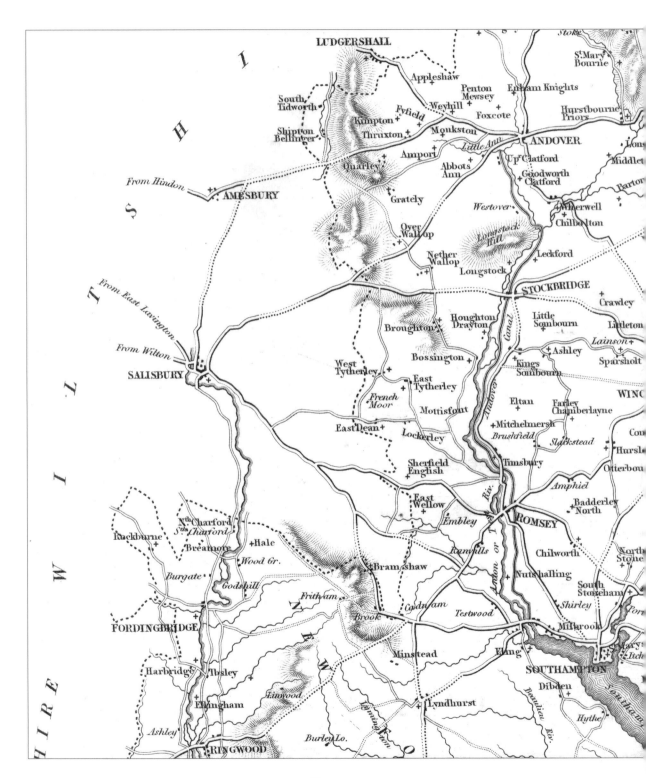

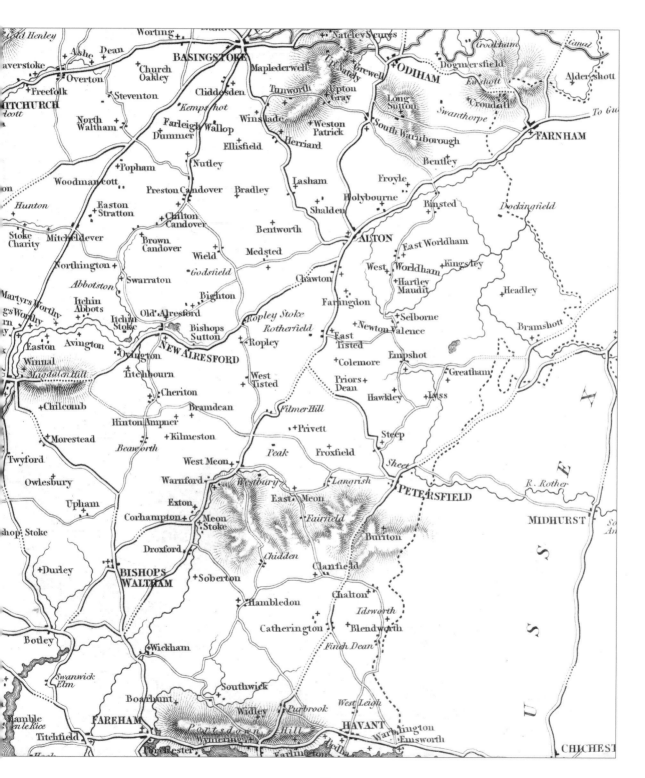

FAIR OAK

Not a great deal is known about the early history of Fair Oak. Relics of the Iron Age, the Roman period and an Anglo-Saxon burial ground have been found, but the name of Fair Oak does not appear on early maps. Originally part of Bishopstoke, it became a separate ecclesiastical parish in 1871 and a civil parish in 1894. There are some 18th-century houses in the Square, although most have been modified or added to. William Cobbett, the political writer who lived near Botley, managed to get the rough track between Botley and Winchester upgraded to the standard of a turnpike road. At first it was called Cobbett Road, but it is now Botley Road. Obviously, the annual fair and the tree in the Square are the sources of the name Fair Oak. In 1936, there was a proposal by the parish council to remove the oak tree in order to improve traffic flow, but villagers objected so strongly that the matter was dropped. Between Bishopstoke and Fair Oak lie Stoke Park Woods. Villagers have 'the liberty of picking snap wood, gathering nuts and flowers and as much fern as they can carry on their backs'. A number of attempts to quash this right have been made, but all have failed. The largest house in the village was at Fair Oak Park. At the beginning of the 20th century, it was owned by George Pember, who is remembered for the considerable contribution he made towards the well-being of the people who lived in the village. There are memorials to the family in the church. After his death, the estate was split up and laid out for new roads and houses. There is also Fair Oak Lodge in Allington Lane, used for a short while as a convent, but now a private school.

FAIR OAK, *The Square c1965* F164017

The oak tree is regarded as the centre of the village. Formerly there was an annual fair supported by the landlord of the ancient Old George Inn (centre). The present tree was planted in 1843, an earlier one having rotted. It is said that parts of it were used to make a seat now in Winchester Cathedral, and also a remarkable, intricate sculpture of the tree and its surroundings which is a feature in the front room of Fair Oak Lodge, now used by the independent King's School.

FAIR OAK
The War Memorial and the Church c1955 F164002

Here we have another view of the oak, with the war memorial placed in front, isolated by road changes. There is also a good view of the Church of St Thomas, dating from 1862. A national school was built in 1867, and children can be seen in the playground. The school closed in 1964, and an old people's home was built on the site. Children now attend schools in Botley Road.

FAIR OAK, *The Church c1955* F164004

This is a closer view of the Church of St Thomas. One might almost call it a utility building. The walls have been constructed of flints (which are copious in the chalk hills of the South Downs) and edged with stone at the windows and doors. The steeply sloping tiled roof is surmounted with ornamental ridge tiles. There is an interesting turret for the one bell. The entrance to the church is from Mortimer Lane on the far side.

FAIR OAK
Eastleigh Road c1955
F164012

This is the old Eastleigh Road, and we can see the post office and the telephone kiosk on the left. We are looking towards the old oak tree, which is just out of sight at the end of the road. Although this one is still used, there is now a new and wider road which leads straight to the main Winchester/Botley Road.

FAIR OAK, *The County Secondary School c1955* F164008

Both the buildings in this picture are part of Fair Oak Junior School. A new ultra-modern building has been constructed as the senior school, which for a time was known as a community school. Under the latest Government changes, it has become Wyvern Technological College. Both schools have been praised after inspections, and the demand for places exceeds those available.

FAIR OAK
Eastleigh Road c1965
F164019

This view shows more clearly houses on the right with the same house that we saw in F164012, page 54, in the centre distance. Note that lines have been painted on the roadway for traffic guidance, but there is still only one footway.

FAIR OAK
The Village c1965
F164016

This road goes to Winchester. To the centre right we can just see the opening of Mortimer Lane, which leads to Bishops Waltham and to Marwell Zoo. There is now on the left a Summerlands Road turning into the old Eastleigh Road to commemorate a long-standing association with the village. The garage is still there, but under new ownership.

EASTLEIGH *from the air 1970* AF203753C

BOTLEY

As one might expect, the Botley Road out of Bishopstoke leads to the picturesque village of Botley with its church, school, and spacious Square with the imposing Market Hall. This is a convenient crossing point of the River Hamble, and there has been a settlement here since at least the 10th century. In 1267, King Henry III granted a charter for a market. William Cobbett, the political writer of the 18th and 19th centuries, best known for his 'Rural Rides', lived for some time nearby. He described the village as 'the most delightful in the world', and added: 'It has everything in a village I love and none of the things I hate'. Flour milling has been carried out in Botley for over a thousand years. Although the mill is still a prominent feature, the business has been transferred recently to a modern factory; a group of small shops now surrounds the old building, which is well worth a visit. Not far away is the old church, no longer in use; it is part of Manor Farm Country Park, where old methods of farming are preserved. There is a railway station some way from the village.

BOTLEY
All Saints' Church
c1955 B544001

Approaching the village from the west along the Botley Road, we see on the right All Saints' Church, built in 1836 in Early English style. The village war memorial is on the left of the picture. Buried in a grave just outside the west end of the church are the parents of Richard St Barbe Baker, founder of the Men of the Trees.

Almost opposite the church is Botley Junior School. It was opened as a National School on 1 January 1856. The building was considerably improved and additions made in 1966, but the outside appearance of the old building was preserved. Note the ornate bargeboards under the roof eaves and the tall chimneys.

BOTLEY, *High Street c1960* B544045

Here we are looking back towards the way we came. In the centre the church stands above the distant houses. Note the house to the centre right: the road has been built up here, and the entrance is now below road level. A low wall gives protection from flooding.

BOTLEY
The Square
c1955 B544011

Again looking back towards the church, this picture gives a good idea of the size of the Square, with the Market Hall on the left. Note the Dolphin Hotel on the left, and the Bugle Inn opposite. Botley once had numerous inns, because it was a kind of coaching station where drivers rested before crossing the Hamble River.

BOTLEY
The Market Hall c1955
B544027

This is another picture of Botley Square, with a good view of the Market Hall. It was built in 1848, and some fifty years later the clock turret and the Tuscan columns were added. There has been a market here since 1267, and the area is now a conservation area. Improvements have been made to the layout of the Square, and renovations are shortly to be made to the Market Hall.

▲ **BOTLEY,** *The Square c1955* B544021

This excellent view of the shops on the side opposite the Market Hall shows an attractive variety of architecture. We have Elcock's, newsagent and tobacconist; Maffey & Son Ltd, ironmongers; then a grocer's shop; and beyond the Bugle Inn another J Maffey & Sons, drapers and outfitters. The one car would find it more difficult to park nowadays.

◀ **BOTLEY**
The Bugle c1960
B544058

A close-up view of the Bugle Inn, a one time coaching inn for travellers before crossing the River Hamble. Note the outside shutters at the windows as well as those next door at Anne Firth's, 'Hair Fashions'.

BOTLEY
The Square c1960
B544067

Here we are looking
east towards the hill
down to the Hamble
River. On the right
we have Robertson,
a chemist, and the
local post office
adding to the many
shopping facilities
for the inhabitants.
The odd thing is that
there are no banks in
the village today.

BOTLEY, *High Street c1955* B544012

Standing out in the distant centre is an attractive house where beer was once sold. It is situated at a crossroads, with
Winchester Road on the left and Church Lane on the right. The corners are awkward to negotiate in modern vehicles.

BOTLEY
Mill Hill c1960
B544051

Here we have a closer view of the house on the crossroads before going down Mill Hill. It has a varied brick pattern for the walls, mullion windows and a tiled roof. Even the outside wall shows an unusual pattern. The windows in the house opposite have been modernised.

BOTLEY, *Winchester Road c1955* B544019

The roads leading out of Botley Square are all narrow; this one leading to Winchester is particularly so. The houses are all of an individual design. Some shops have encroached into this road.

BOTLEY
Church Lane
c1955 B544028

Another view of Church Lane, with some older cottages along with some rural gardens, just the kind one may expect to see in the country. Off Church Lane it is possible to see Hamble Quay, a small area where boats using the River Hamble could moor after deliveries to the flour mill.

◄ BOTLEY
Church Lane
c1955 B544010

Church Lane leads
to the original
Botley church,
now part of the
Manor Farm com-
plex of buildings
and used for other
purposes. The lane
is narrow and has
its attractive, indi-
vidually designed
houses which
appealed so much
to William Cobbett
and, indeed, to
others who see
them today.

▲ *detail from* B544005

► BOTLEY
Mill Hill c1955
B544005

We are at the bot-
tom of the hill look-
ing back towards
the Square. The
ornamental rail-
ings on the right
are those of Botley
Mill. There was once
a memorial stone
on the left back-
ing onto the home,
now demolished, of
William Cobbett, but
it was thought to be
in too dangerous a
position and is now
in the square.

▼ *detail from* B544006

BOTLEY
The YMCA International Youth Camp c1955
B544015

William Cobbett came to Botley in 1805 and purchased the Fairthorns Estate, comprising 300 acres. In later life he became bankrupt, and the land was sold. In 1854, Fairthorne Manor was built. After belonging to various owners it was purchased by the YMCA, and has become an international training centre with many and varied courses available for young people of all ages and nationalities.

◄ **BOTLEY**
The Mills c1950
B544006

This is an excellent view of Botley Mills, which produced cattle fodder and seed for farmers. Note how low barges could come up under the mills for unloading and refilling. The water in front of the mill has now been covered over and has become a car park. The mill is no longer in use, but has moved into a modern building not far away. Now there are shops around the mill.

► **BOTLEY**
The Railway Hotel and Station Entrance c1960 B544059

Botley Station (entrance on the left of the photograph), which is approached via Mill Hill, is well outside the village. One descends to it from a road bridge. Once used for the distribution of strawberries in the season, it is still in use. The Railway Hotel opposite also still exists, but is used mainly as a local pub.

CHANDLER'S FORD

Just as Botley is to the south east of old Eastleigh, so Chandler's Ford is to the north west. Its development has been roughly on the same time-scale as Eastleigh. Originally, that is to say before c1900, a collection of small farms slowly added dwellings and became hamlets, which subsequently joined together in a variety of ways. Chandler's Ford is situated on the turnpike road between Southampton and Winchester and thence on to London; on both sides there is a hill to descend, and Monk's Brook has be crossed by a ford or later by a bridge. This stream could be not much more than a trickle, making the immediate area swampy and unpleasant, but after rain it might develop a strong flow with flooding for a considerable width. On the Winchester side there was a coaching station at Fryern Hill (other spellings to be found on maps are Fishers Hill and Fernhill) with the Halfway Inn, which in earlier times had a signpost bearing the coat of arms of Winchester and of Southampton. On the Southampton side there is the Hut, originally a farm lying well back from the road, but in due course the settlement came forward to establish an inn, now a Beefeater.

An important feature of the area was the brick industry. The underlying clay was made into some of the finest bricks in country - some were even exported abroad. A community developed, with large houses for the managers and a row of smaller cottages for the brick makers. The railway station, which opened in 1849, was an added attraction, enabling easy dispersal of the bricks. For a couple of years there was a successful racecourse nearby, and the station platforms were lengthened to cope with the wagons bringing the racing horses. Unfortunately, the unpredictable nature of the soil - iron-hard or boggy - brought a promising venture to an end.

◄ **CHANDLER'S FORD**
The Parade c1960 C490074

This is the shopping parade, with shops to meet the everyday needs of the local inhabitants. As in Eastleigh, the ground floors of houses have been converted. An unseen advantage is that they all have cellars, as the ground slopes away behind. The hexagonal building at the bottom was a pro- vision store plus post office, then a gas company showroom for a short time, and finally Martin's Central Heating, before it was demolished for road widening.

Later, the area was regarded as an attractive place in which to live. Large houses were built - one had thirteen bedrooms with dressing room attached - and between the First and Second World Wars a large part of Chandler's Ford became a dormitory for directors, professors and the like working in Southampton. In 1932, when it was proposed to add Chandler's Ford to Eastleigh, there was strong opposition, and three of the opposers were elected to the council. Subsequently, the merger was accepted, and one of the protesters became mayor of the borough.

▶ **CHANDLER'S FORD**
The Parade c1965
C490064

Another view of the Parade, showing Lowmans, baker; Lloyds Bank; Jenkins, newsagent and tobacconist; National Provincial Bank; Dews, children's clothing; and an estate agent. Most of these shops are still there, although some have changed their nature. The National Provincial has moved across the road to join the Westminster Bank.

◀ **CHANDLER'S FORD**
Bournemouth Road c1960 C490065

We are approaching Chandler's Ford from Southampton along Bournemouth Road, altered from Southampton Road to avoid confusion with another road of that name. Hendy's had a large works in Southampton, but seeing the potential in Chandler's Ford, the firm opened a garage. After the Second World War it moved its works to this site, closing the petrol service station and developing a large showroom and repair shop. Apparently, the move has been successful, as Hendy Ltd has recently put forward plans for considerable development, possibly moving to the site to be vacated by Manor Bakeries (see page 39).

CHANDLER'S FORD
The Parade c1960
C490075

This is the view from the other end of the Parade. Much to the satisfaction of shop-keepers, car parking, as shown here, is still allowed. Carey & Lambert's Austin garage (centre right) has long since gone, as has the Chandler's Ford School seen in the distant centre of the photograph.

◄ CHANDLER'S FORD
Bournemouth Road c1960 C490092

Here we are looking at shops on the side opposite the Parade. Wainwright the chemist's (right) is an old Eastleigh firm that until recently survived in the centre of the town, but this branch has become a showroom for heating appliances. The taller building standing out from the building line is the former Westminster Bank, and the smaller building is still the Chandler's Ford Post Office.

▲ **CHANDLER'S FORD,** *Bournemouth Road c1965* C490093

This view shows the same buildings as C490092 from the other end, showing clearly the Westminster Bank before its amalgamation with the National Provincial to become NatWest. Then comes the Co-op shop, later converted into a shop for a travel agent and a small food shop. The Co-operative Movement, once so strong in the railway town of Eastleigh, disappeared from the area not long after this photograph was taken. Note again that convenient car parking is permitted.

◀ **CHANDLER'S FORD**
The Shopping Precinct c1965 C490121

The shopping precinct was built when it was thought that the shopping centre for the growing suburb would be here. It is hardly attractive in design; the entrance is between the two buildings shown here, and leads to a square surrounded by small shops. It was not popular, and tradesmen did not stay long. Waitrose applied to open a store, but the plans were rejected by the council. There are now plans to upgrade the precinct.

▼ **CHANDLER'S FORD,** *Hursley Road c1965* C490117

The Railway Hotel, near the Chandler's Ford station, changed its name to the Monks Brook Inn after the closure of the station in 1969. The name remains, although the station has been reopened. The road leads to the village of Hursley, and all this area was once part of the Hursley Manor Estate. The service station on the left is now a car showroom. Immediately behind was the long established firm of Dean & Son, suppliers of garden materials. Sad to say, there is now a large block of flats on the site.

CHANDLER'S FORD
Common Road
c1965 C490119

Common Road was one of the early developments. It comes off Hursley Road, and descends to a stream crossed by a ford where the water might be so deep that food suppliers could not get across. The road has a pleasing variety of house styles, often with long gardens in front.

◄ **CHANDLER'S FORD**
Winchester Road
c1965 C490302

We are now back at the junction with Hursley Road where Bournemouth Road becomes Winchester Road. We can see part of the old post office, now a heating and plumbing shop (left), and the entrance to the precinct on the right. A considerable change has taken place here, with a large roundabout being constructed on the post office site. A No 47 Hants & Dorset bus is on its way from Winchester to Southampton, a regular service which still runs, albeit with the livery of Solent Blue.

► **CHANDLER'S FORD**
Bodycoats Road
c1960 C490076

Just beyond the precinct, a builder named Trickett built an estate of bungalows with Bodycoats Road through the centre. Right at the top in the centre can be seen some of the buildings of Fryern Hill Hospital, an isolation hospital well out of Eastleigh when it was built in 1912. It is now demolished, and modern houses have been built on the site.

CHANDLER'S FORD
The Sanatorium c1955
C490007

This is another hospital recently demolished; it has been replaced by 95 homes. It was built in 1900 as a workhouse for the Hursley District Council at the northern end of Hursley Road. Transferred to Chandler's Ford, it became a sanatorium and later a psychiatric unit for teenagers, which has now moved to Winchester. A book has been published giving the story of Leigh House.

CHANDLER'S FORD, *Merdon Avenue c1955* C490014

William Wallis (responsible for the Eagle Building in Eastleigh) had the bright idea of creating an 'Inland Bournemouth' on a triangle of land between Hursley Road, Winchester Road and Brownhill Road. A number of large houses with spacious grounds were built, but most are now converted into flats. Merdon Avenue, originally named The Crescent, was a continuation of the idea, but with rather smaller 'large houses'.

CHANDLER'S FORD
The Primary School c1965 C490135

The first school in Chandler's Ford was in Hursley Road near St Boniface Church; it moved to a more substantial building in Bournemouth Road, but eventually the Junior School was located to a site off Merdon Avenue. Landscaping has cancelled out the rather bleak look of the school, shown here not long after it opened in 1956. It is now called Merdon School.

CHANDLER'S FORD, *Sherborne House School c1955* C490006

Sherborne House School was established in 1933 by Mrs E Wise, whose family came from Sherborne in Dorset. It is a day preparatory school with about 175 pupils for girls aged 3 to 11 and boys aged 3 to 8. It is in delightfully wooded grounds of four acres. There are extensions to the original house in Lakewood Road with facilities for sport and music.

▼ **CHANDLER'S FORD,** *Hiltingbury Road c1960* C490043

Hiltingbury Road leads from Winchester Road to Hiltingbury Common, which during the Second World War and for some time after was covered with huts and used for various purposes - British troops, American troops, prisoners of war and eventually homes for Poles who had escaped to England, and who are now absorbed into the Eastleigh community.

CHANDLER'S FORD
Hursley Road c1955
C490008

Part of Hiltingbury Common was used after the war to accommodate soldiers and their families who had nowhere to live. It was near to Hocomb Road, and known No 17 Families Camp – note the signpost to it on the right. Facilities at the camp were more than tolerable, and some families were reluctant to move away.

◄ **CHANDLER'S FORD**
*Hiltingbury Road
Shops c1965* C490127

In due course, all the military installations were cleared from Hiltingbury Common; the area was developed into a large housing estate on one side and a recreation ground on the other. Hiltingbury Road was upgraded from a track and went through to Hursley Road. A shopping parade was built, as we see here.

► **CHANDLER'S FORD**
*Ashdown Road
c1965* C490129

Near the end of Hiltingbury Road, and on a corner with a new Ashdown Road, a public house called the Tabby Cat was built and thrived for some time. However, it has been demolished recently and replaced with flats. The houses, flats and shops in Ashdown Road are seen in this photograph.

CHANDLER'S FORD
The Hiltingbury/Kingsway Crossroads, Kingsway Post Office c1964 C490031

Historians are of the opinion that when the forester Purkiss took the body of William Rufus to Winchester, he must have travelled through or near Chandler's Ford, and roads here have been given the names of some of those involved. For instance, there is a Kingsway which crosses Hiltingbury Road at this particularly wide crossroads. Unfortunately, Kingsway Post Office has been closed.

CHANDLER'S FORD
Lake Road c1955
C490024

Lake Road, with houses overlooking the main lake, is undoubtedly a delightful place to live. Away from the traffic and not too near the lake edge, the trees, the bushes and the grassy slopes make it an ideal area for watching bird and other types of wildlife.

CHANDLER'S FORD
The Lake c1955
C490022

Chandler's Ford Lake has been much improved since this photograph was taken. The water seeps through from higher ground and is held back by a concrete dam, and below it is a water garden, once a feature of Merdon Court. It has been reconstructed recently. It is possible that this lake, along with the one in Cranbury Park and the site of Merdon School, were once monks' fish ponds.

CHANDLER'S FORD
Marlborough Road c1960 C490037

Such was the attraction of Hiltingbury Common that a number of roads were cut through the woodlands, and large houses were built here with reasonably large gardens in a pleasant woodland setting. At first, the roads were rough and there was little control of traffic, as we can see in this view of Marlborough Road.

CHANDLER'S FORD
Oakwood Road c1960 C490042

All these roads are similar. The rough roads have all been paved. Almost all the houses are detached, and often individually designed. The Local Area Committee of the Borough Council is doing its best to maintain the special ambiance of the district. However, it is a sad fact that developers are beginning to nibble at any open spaces for the building of flats. There is a Tree Preservation Order covering this area, which we may hope will prevent the destruction of most of the trees.

CHANDLER'S FORD
Gordon Road c1960 C490057

▲ **CHANDLER'S FORD**
Nichol Road
c1960 C490059

◄ **CHANDLER'S FORD**
Randall Road
c1965 C490111

▼ **CHANDLER'S FORD**
Western Road
c1965 C490102

CHANDLER'S FORD
Hocombe Road c1955 C490036

Hocombe Road is the northern boundary of Hiltingbury, and indeed of the borough. It is also the boundary of Cranbury Park, the Chamberlayne family estate. Note that mature trees separate the footway from the roadway. This is probably the route along which the body of William Rufus was taken to Winchester. Unfortunately, the proximity of the M3 motorway has led to an increase in traffic along this formerly quiet road.

INDEX

NAMES OF SUBSCRIBERS

The following people have kindly supported this book by subscribing to copies before publication.

The Alexander Family, Eastleigh

For Dean Allen and Family

For Lloyd Allen and Family

The Allen Family, Bishopstoke 2005

Albert Ayles, Eastleigh

The Baldwin Family, Ontario, Canada

To Joyce Barrett, Love From Ted & Carol

W J Bates

The Batten Family, Eastleigh

George Bazeley

Happy Anniversary Sam and Gary Beattie

Mr K C Bennett & Mrs E Bennett

The Bennett Family, Bishopstoke

The Berry Family, Eastleigh

The Bibbo Family, Botley and Eastleigh

P J Blaxall and J C Blaxall, Chandler's Ford

For Derek Boggust on his 80th birthday

Gloria and Peter Bond, Chandler's Ford

The Broom Family, Bishopstoke

For my Brother, Andrew Brown

For my Father, George Brown

In Memory of Mollie Brown, Bishopstoke

Ronald and Jade Bull, Fair Oak

In Memory of William & Emily Bushrod

Michael Charles and Ann Veronica Butt

Geraldene Cardwell, Dez Cardwell

Stephen Carter

Percy and Doris Chandler, Eastleigh

Philip Clements, Chandler's Ford

Stephen Clements, Chandler's Ford

Colin and Pat Compton, Bideford, Devon

Harold and Barbara Corbin, Eastleigh

The Family of Corey-Vincent-Marshall

David Wallace Cottrell, Fair Oak

Joyce Dacombe

Ann Denyer

Mr and Mrs R Dorman, Eastleigh

In Memory Of My Husband Ron, Love Dorothy

The Elsey Family

Mike, Beryl, Karen and Derek Fay, Eastleigh

Thelma and Eddie Fearn, Golden Anniversary

Barbara and Allan Ferris, Chandler's Ford, Hampshire

Joan Field, Eastleigh

William Field, Eastleigh

The Fitzgerald Family, Bishopstoke

Mr R and Mrs P Foyle, Eastleigh

Lin and Ron Gamblin, Pearl Anniversary

Mr R W and Mrs M A Gerrard, Bishopstoke

In Memory of our sons Ian and John Gilham

The Glasspool Family, Bishopstoke

Pat Godfrey, née Dennis, In Memory of Roy

Victor G Goldsmith, Eastleigh

Happy birthday, Keith Green 2005

Pamela Mary Grinyer, formerly of Kingsway

The Grout Family, Eastleigh Borough

Mr B J and Mrs E K Hanley, Bishopstoke

Peter A Hardy

The Haskell Family of Locksley Road

M H Hayter; Michael H Hayter, Bishopstoke

Betty & Mike Hill, Desborough Rd 1961-90

In Memory of Florence Ireland, 1907-2002

Mr G P & Mrs C M Ives, Eastleigh

Dear Nanny and Grandad, Thank you, Jade

Fluffy Lou and Jay Jay, Bishopstoke

Steve, Anniversary Wishes, Love Jenny

Dominic Morgan Jones, Chandler's Ford

Mr B J and Mrs M J Killick, Bishopstoke

Mrs M Knox

The Legg Family, Riverside, Bishopstoke

Linda, Happy 29th Birthday

The Lipscombe Family, Bishopstoke

The Lock Family, Bishopstoke

Lloyd Maclachlan
The Macneish Family, Eastleigh
The McCabe Family, Eastleigh
Mr Simon McCormick, Fair Oak, Eastleigh
Mr A and Mrs S McCoye, Bishopstoke
Clive & Linda McLellan of Bishopstoke
Derek and Heather Manaton, Fair Oak
Peter George Miller
The Neal Family, Eastleigh
Steve, Lyn & Alice Nicholls
Mrs Daphne North, Bishopstoke
Oakwood Dental Practise, Botley
Brian and Peggy O'Neill, Eastleigh
Michael and Carole O'Neill, Morton in Marsh
The Owens Family, Bishopstoke
Mr J Padwick, Bishopstoke
Brian and Janet Painter of Fair Oak
For my Sister, Sally Painter
Grace Jane Palmer, Eastleigh
Samuel Marc Palmer, Eastleigh
Anne and Bill Parker, Bishopstoke
Margaret and Paul of Chandler's Ford
F R Payne and Family
The James Pearce Family, Campbell Rd, Eastleigh
To My Dad, Stephen Penn, With Love, Cheryl
In Memory of Norman Phillips, Eastleigh
R A E Phillips (Cutter), Eastleigh
Mr C M and Mrs P M Pitcher, Eastleigh
To Anthony & Betty Powlesland, From Julie
In Memory Of My Wife, Lilian R Rabbetts
The Ralph Family of Fair Oak
Colin Richards

Graham R Riley, Eastleigh
In Memory of W Rogers, Bishopstoke
The Ruffell Family, Eastleigh
The Scott Family, Chandler's Ford
In Memory of Bill & Michael Sharpe
Chris & Wendy Shehan
Wendy and Michael Sleeman, Chandler's Ford
In Memory of Reginald and Cicely Smith
In Memory of Samuel and Dorothy Smith
Lisa Lee and Lauren Smith, Chandler's Ford
To Roy Smith From Maureen, Xmas 2005
June E Steele, Fair Oak
The Stent Family, Bishopstoke, Eastleigh
The Stephens Family, Eastleigh
David & Ann Stubbs, Chandler's Ford
The Family of F C Stubington
The Tarlton Family, Fair Oak
John Thurman, Eastleigh
Ron Ticehurst, Eastleigh
G W Upton and B D Upton
The Vickers Family, Eastleigh
M and E Walden, Chandler's Ford
The Waldrons, Mortimer Lane, Fairoak
The Warry Family, Leigh Road, Eastleigh
Mr K J West and Mrs R E West, Eastleigh
In memory of A G White, Local Builder
The Whitfield Family, Eastleigh since 1900
Peter J Wildsmith, Eastleigh
Paul Windsor, Eastleigh
The Winter Family, Bishopstoke
Happy Memories, Ron Wood, J P, Eastleigh
To Anne Worsfold on her 70th birthday

FRITH PRODUCTS & SERVICES

Francis Frith would doubtless be pleased to know that the pioneering publishing venture he started in 1860 still continues today. Over a hundred and forty years later, The Francis Frith Collection continues in the same innovative tradition and is now one of the foremost publishers of vintage photographs in the world. Some of the current activities include:

Interior Decoration

Today Frith's photographs can be seen framed and as giant wall murals in thousands of pubs, restaurants, hotels, banks, retail stores and other public buildings throughout the country. In every case they enhance the unique local atmosphere of the places they depict and provide reminders of gentler days in an increasingly busy and frenetic world.

Product Promotions

Frith products are used by many major companies to promote the sales of their own products or to reinforce their own history and heritage. Frith promotions have been used by Hovis bread, Courage beers, Scots Porage Oats, Colman's mustard, Cadbury's foods, Mellow Birds coffee, Dunhill pipe tobacco, Guinness, and Bulmer's Cider.

Genealogy and Family History

As the interest in family history and roots grows world-wide, more and more people are turning to Frith's photographs of Great Britain for images of the towns, villages and streets where their ancestors lived; and, of course, photographs of the churches and chapels where their ancestors were christened, married and buried are an essential part of every genealogy tree and family album.

Frith Products

All Frith photographs are available Framed or just as Mounted Prints and Posters (size 23 x 16 inches). These may be ordered from the address below. From time to time other products - Address Books, Maps, etc - are available.

The Internet

Already ninety thousand Frith photographs can be viewed and purchased on the internet through the Frith websites and a myriad of partner sites.

For more detailed information on Frith companies and products, look at these sites:

www.francisfrith.co.uk
www.francisfrith.com
(for North American visitors)

See the complete list of Frith Books at:

www.francisfrith.co.uk

This web site is regularly updated with the latest list of publications from The Francis Frith Collection. If you wish to buy books relating to another part of the country that your local bookshop does not stock, you may purchase on-line.

For further information, trade, or author enquiries please contact us at the address below:
The Francis Frith Collection, Frith's Barn, Teffont, Salisbury, Wiltshire, England SP3 5QP.
Tel: +44 (0)1722 716 376 Fax: +44 (0)1722 716 881 Email: sales@francisfrith.co.uk

See Frith books on the internet at www.francisfrith.co.uk